THIS COULD BE THE START OF SOMETHING STUPID

A Book for Love and Laughter

THE CARTOON BANK, INC.

A FIRESIDE BOOK

PUBLISHED BY SIMON & SCHUSTER

New York   London   Toronto   Sydney   Tokyo   Singapore

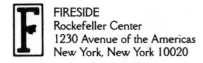

FIRESIDE
Rockefeller Center
1230 Avenue of the Americas
New York, New York 10020

FIRESIDE and colophon are registered trademarks of Simon & Schuster Inc.

Designed by Folio Graphics Co., Inc.

Manufactured in the United States of America

10   9   8   7   6   5   4   3   2   1

Library of Congress Cataloging-in-Publication Data

This could be the start of something stupid : a book for love and
laughter / The Cartoon Bank, Inc.
    p.   cm.
   1. Love—Caricatures and cartoons.   2. Marriage—Caricatures and
cartoons.   3. American wit and humor, Pictorial.   I. Cartoon Bank, Inc.
NC1428.T48   1995
741.5'973—dc20   94-37953
                                          CIP

ISBN 0-671-87957-X

Original cartoons and reprints of individual cartoons are available through The
Cartoon Bank, 495 Warburton Avenue, Hastings on Hudson, New York 10706;
tel: (914) 478-5527; fax: (914) 478-5604

Contributors to
THIS COULD BE THE START OF SOMETHING STUPID

George Abbott

M. K. Brown

Frank Cotham

Michael Crawford

Leo Cullum

Boris Drucker

Ed Frascino

Mort Gerberg

Anne Gibbons

Liz Haberfeld

William Haefeli

Marian Henley

John Jonik

Bruce Eric Kaplan

Arnie Levin

Robert Mankoff

Huguette Martel

Michael Maslin

Heather McAdams

P. S. Mueller

John O'Brien

Libby Reid

Brian Savage

Bernard Schoenbaum

Danny Shanahan

David Sipress

Mick Stevens

P. C. Vey

Dean Vietor

Jack Ziegler

About the Cartoon Bank

The Cartoon Bank is an electronic cartoon stock house featuring more than 20,000 cartoons by *The New Yorker* cartoonists and others. Cartoon CD-ROMs, cartoons on disk, printing rights, custom cartoons, books, cards, limited-edition prints and original artwork are all available for purchase. To order any of the cartoons in this collection, or to receive a free selection of cartoons on any topic by fax, call 1-800-897-TOON or e-mail CartoonBnk@AOL.com.

A Message from the President
(OF THE CARTOON BANK)

My fellow Americans, as Commander in Chief of the Cartoon Bank, I've dispatched a corps of cartoonists to the front lines of love and these courageous satirists have brought back *This Could Be the Start of Something Stupid.*

While this book does not offer health security, or even social security, it does put humor security right in your own love-starved hands.

This book shows that, while the Cold War is over, the war between, and even among, the sexes is heating up, boiling over, and causing a huge mess that has to be dealt with. I'm considering a superfund for toxic relationships but, as a stopgap, here are 120 flagrantly funny cartoons that produce such paroxysms of pleasure that they make relationships largely unnecessary.

So, give this book to someone you love. Then have them give it to someone they love, and so on. Eventually, you may get it back again. In the meantime buy yourself another book and, for god's sake, this time hold on to it!

Thank you, and you, and you, and especially you, sweetheart.

Bob Mankoff
PRESIDENT
THE CARTOON BANK

Even though he wanted to make a good impression on his first date with Mary Lou Durren, Farley made a point to arrive thirteen minutes late. "I don't want to set a precedent for punctuality."

"Hi, I'm Jon Reddekop, and this is my wife, Pam, on rhythm guitar."

11

"*You* handle the social graces. *I'm* just going to drink."

15

16

17

"We just have terrible timing. When I was between marriages and available you were doing three to five in Allenwood."

19

GIRL'S EYE VIEW...

BOY'S EYE VIEW...

WHO THE HELL KNOWS?

DOES HE HAVE ANOTHER GIRLFRIEND? DOES HE HAVE A BIG ONE? A YEAST INFECTION? HERPES? DEATH? IS THIS WORTH IT? WILL HE EVER CALL ME AGAIN? IF I DON'T, WILL HE EVER CALL ME AGAIN? IF I DO, DON'T SELL YOURSELF CHEAP. MAYBE I DON'T WANT TO WET PANTIES HAVE NO BRAINS. WHERE'S MY DIAPHRAGM? YOU DON'T HAVE TO PET TO BE POPULAR IS IT WORTH THE TROUBLE? I CAN'T—MY THIGHS ARE TOO FAT HOW'S MY BREATH? MAYBE WE SHOULD JUST BE FRIENDS COULD THIS BE TRUE LOVE?

LIBBY REID

"You're still the king of the apes as far as I'm concerned, dear."

" 'Damned if I know' is not my favorite expression. It's just that you keep asking me questions to which 'damned if I know' is the appropriate answer."

"I have a weakness for men who have a weakness for women who have a weakness for individually foil-wrapped chocolate-covered cherries."

"I was certain that one day these boots would walk all over him, but, damn it, they never did."

29

"Mother, what do you mean the happiest day of my life?
I'm only twenty-three."

"I would *never* marry an actor."

"Actually, we met through the personals column. That's my ad."

"More than one woman has had to talk to her psychiatrist about me."

SIPRESS

"And just remember: Daddy got you out of that nasty pet store because he hopes you'll act really cute and friendly in the park, especially around attractive, single women."

"It's amazing. We've just met, but I feel we've known each other since we were kids, became high school sweethearts, got married too young, had a bunch of brats, went through a messy divorce, reconciled, remarried each other, and are now back together again after all these years."

35

TIME, THE GREAT HEALER

LIBBY REID

37

"Yes, Dave and I are separated. He's living in the past."

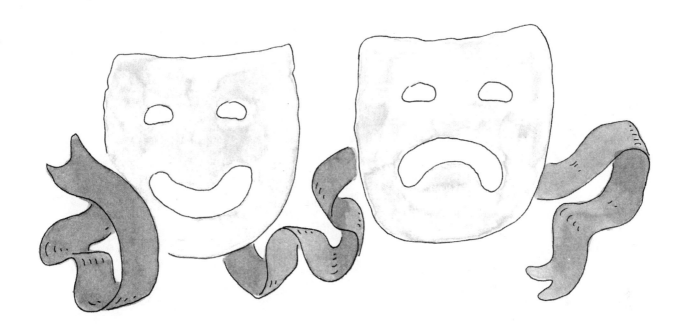

"I'm pregnant!"

"The attitude problem at this party is ferocious."

"You're not the Roger Dennison I married!" "Right! I'm Al Potts."

" 'Yippie-ti-yo-ki-yay'? Is that all you ever have to say?"

"I'd like to find a man who is sensitive in general,
and macho in emergencies."

"I don't know how you can ever hope to be politically correct if you keep disagreeing with me."

"I think what I'm really looking for is a woman who'd be happy with only *one* last name."

"Believe me, I was *not* giving you the eye. I was staring at you in disbelief."

"It's only fair to warn you. I can't handle one-to-one relationships."

"I knew the marriage was over when he taped *Star Trek* over our wedding video."

Helen Loomis, Paparazzi Wife

MAJOR HEARTBREAK RECOVERY SCHEDULE

"After twelve years of marriage a woman develops a kind of sixth sense about when her husband wants to leave a party."

"Marry you? Why, I wouldn't even vote to let you into my co-op."

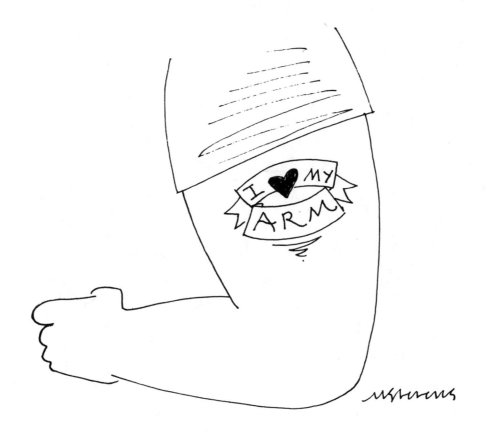

"And, to every one's amazement, do you, Anne, take Harold to be your lawfully wedded husband?"

"I want to thank you, Brenda, for being such a cheap date."

"My first husband, Ralph, had an acute interest in the paranormal. Then one day he burst into flames. Edward likes gardening."

"You know, sometimes I almost wish you were back in real estate."

"Shouldn't we be videotaping this?"

"Thanks to all those self-help books you made me read, I realized
I'm too good for you."

" 'A book of verses beneath the bough, a jug of wine, a loaf of bread, and'—Oh, there's my phone."

"Sex? I thought you said you wanted a sax!"

"Just because your name is Dolly it doesn't mean I'm going to sing 'Hello, Dolly!' every time you come down the goddamn stairs. You knew that when you married me."

BLIND DATE

"He was a class act, but that's all it was—an act."

"What do you mean, I remind you of your wife? I am your wife."

73

So! You're having a mad, passionate love affair. But haven't you forgotten about someone near and dear?

Your cat wants you back.

78

"Before you go, perhaps you'd be interested in purchasing one of our 'Frank and Myra' T-Shirts or coffee mugs."

So what's it like being married to Mark all these years?

I love it!

It's not easy to keep a relationship fresh, alive and exciting...

but it beats pumping life into blind dates.

80

"I know you miss your wife, but I wish you'd stop calling me Ethel!"

83

"I'm Kurt. This brochure will explain the rest."

"Listen, your new identity may fool the mob, but to me you're still the same old shifty Leo you always were."

"Remember when you and I fought over Harry, the love of our lives?"
"Who won?"

"OK, let's compromise: First we'll talk about baseball and then we'll talk about our relationship!"

87

88

"What ever happened to quiche, and the men that ate it?"

"See, it's right here in the pre-nup, Louise; if you walk out,
I get two weeks severance sex."

"Let's face it Lester. The sole basis for our entire relationship
is my air-conditioning."

"We both called the wind 'Mariah.' At the time it seemed like enough."

WHAT SHE SAID:

WHAT HE HEARD:

LIBBY REID

"Cut the comedy, Ann! Get dressed! We're late!"

"How about if I come over and wash my hair *with* you."

"Look, don't try to weasel out of this. It was my dream, but you
had the affair in it."

JONIK

"OK, I'm a feminist. Now will you sleep with me?"

Wasting Time

"I can only suggest you do a series of exercises to strengthen your abdominal muscles, Mitch. I can't do them for you."

Searching for Mr. REALLY Right
Women Seeking Men
RAVISHING
DID YOU love "Thelma & Louise"? Believe Anita? Disappointed in Woody? You could be the MAN FOR ME!!! x 3122
ATTRACTIVE SAF ISO
x 3211
GORGEOUS DHF
SBF
DAF se
x 40
ACTI
x 2111
x 2231
© Anne Gibbons

"Natalie, you know my world revolves around you constantly, except, of course, on Tuesdays and Wednesdays, major holidays, and every other weekend."

"What do you mean, this is just like the one he bought for my daughter?
We don't have a daughter."

"I've been waiting three weeks for Herb to call, so I can tell him never to call me again."

"Yoo hoo! Sweetheart! Have we forgotten? It's Mardi Gras Night!"

"I'm working, Kyle. Don't Peter Pan me."

"We've had our disagreements before, dear, but this is the first time you've ever called me a security risk."

"Joanne? Oh! I was hoping to get your answering machine."

"I never allow anyone to contradict me on the first date."

"He came into my life suddenly one day in 1992. Then, one day, just as suddenly, he left."

Maggie has just met the Man of Her Dreams...

Unfortunately, she's his Woman of the Week.

THIS IS ONLY A **TEST** ARE YOU **BITTER?** FOR THOSE WHO'VE HAD IT UP TO HERE WITH THE VERY OPPOSITE SEX

BITTER WOMAN TEST

T F — The quickest way to a man's heart is a Knife in his back

T F — Men are all wimpy, amoral, whining, cheapskates

T F — Men are pond scum, only slimier

T F — Men are far too ridiculously proud of the "Little Hitler" that lives in their pants

BITTER MAN TEST

T	F	
☐	☐	Take away their cosmetics, high heels and trick clothes and all you have are naked women
☐	☐	Women are money-sucking big-butt crybabies
☐	☐	They are sneaky, squeaky, pea-brained sperm thieves
☐	☐	They're a pack of bossy frigid sluts

YOUR BITTER SCORE: You and an equivalent scorer of the opposite sex will spend a weekend together locked in a tiny, sound-proof rubber room!

LIBBY REID